Astrology: Discover the Power of Zodiac Signs: Discover Your Deepest Life Purpose, Find Your Soul Mate, and Learn How to Stop Worrying About the Future

by S.J. Morgan

Table of Contents

Your Free Gift

As a special thank you for downloading and purchasing this book I would like to offer you an exclusive free eBook about "Law of Attraction 101" which I believe can personally help anybody achieve their dreams.

If you want to take your life to another level, and become the ultimate manifester and truly learn the stepping blocks of mastering the law of attraction then this guide book will help tremendously.

In this free eBook you will learn the 25 little steps that can bring you massive results

>>> __DOWNLOAD THIS FREE EBOOK BY CLICKING HERE__<<<

Law of
Attraction 101

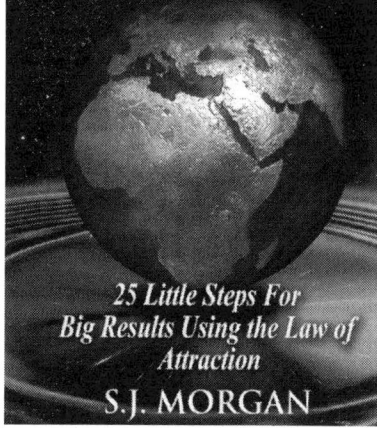

25 Little Steps For
Big Results Using the Law of
Attraction

S.J. MORGAN

Introduction

Astrology is an extensively wide subject. It interests some and bewilders others! This subject has many variations. In the sense, every culture has a different type of astrology to follow, but interestingly it is perceived with similar understanding across the globe. Some people see astrology as a unit of religion, while some think of it to be spiritual. Nevertheless, it can very well be termed as a branch of science because no astrological prediction is done without a logical reasoning.

There is a reason, probably a very strong reason for everything happening around. Let's make it sound a little simpler. Astrology basically tries to establish a direct relation between you and the constantly changing planetary positions. Right from the time of your birth, till you take the last breath of your life, these planets will keep having different effects on you. Every situation will be different in your life and in case, if anything repeats; the results will always be different.

People who want to believe in astrology will believe it no matter what. When we start experiencing extraordinary things, we tend to think more about it and a time comes when we are completely ready to rely on it. By extraordinary, we do not mean anything supernatural. It can be anything that we tend to ignore in the normal course of our lives. It can be an extremely ordinary situation too that we have been taking for granted for long. Believe it or not, astrology does help us to have a better understanding of the world we are living in. We tend to understand the people we live or work with more deeply. Imagine, if we could understand the reason behind everything, wouldn't be all of us happy and contented?

The strongest tool in astrology is horoscope. Any practitioner of Astrology who has in depth knowledge and experience can read a horoscope and tell what kind of personality, nature or character that particular person has. He will know the in and out of a person.

That actually sounds scary but it is interesting too! If this is not enough then here is more for you. A good horoscope reader will also predict some instances that may take place in your life at some point or the other. Many astrologers avoid telling about the mishaps (future) if any though because that is considered to be against the ethics of this line of study. But, there are many who just go ahead and inform about it to the concerned person as they feel, it will keep him or her aware as well as precautioned.

We see many people relying on astrological predictions these days. The last decade saw an extensive growth of followers as far as astrology is concerned. We cannot answer why because it is more related to the faith factor. You have faith on it, you believe it. It is that straightforward a thing! Famous people, including movie stars, politicians, bureaucrats and people from other industries have found a strong faith in this science may be because they experienced the power the astrology has!

Astrology and Elements

Future is indeterminate! Nobody is acquainted with the happenings just after a few seconds! In fact everyone is anxious about future and wants to know the occurrence, precautions & protection and remedies to stay healthy and happy. For this, Astrology is the Key to open the past and prospects of hidden treasures and tragic of our life.

Astrology emerged from 'astro' denoting 'stars' and 'logos' symbolizes 'language', together connotes the 'language of stars'. Astrology is the sacred and ancient science of relating the maneuver of planets with the people and revealing their life.

What are the four elements?

Tradition views the entire universe consisting of four elements that represents the basic traits and emphasis on horoscope. The emphasis or non-emphasis of elements in the individual horoscope explores fundamental aspects of personality. The four elements of astrology refer to the imperative energies that make up the whole creation comprehended by human beings.

The astrological birth chart begins from the first breath of people. The elements in the birth chart reveal the energy patterns and vibratory manifestations. The mix of these elements in your birth chart throws light on individual's nature and life lessons.

The four elements that are the basic principles of life are— Fire, Earth, Air and Water. Each of the elements corresponds to a basic kind of energy and consciousness that operates within everyone.

Elements and Sign

According to the chronicles, 'Ptolemy' is ascribed in making the correlation between the four elements and the signs of astrology by assigning three zodiacal signs to each element in the 2nd century AD. The zodiacal wheel consisting of twelve signs reflected the balance of four elements.

The individual is strongly accustomed to the element of any sign and contains consciousness and mode of perception accordingly. The elements of the signs are denoted by color. Fire which is red indicates spirit or identity, earth is green saying practicality, air is found black with intellectual & social matters and water which is blue specify emotions and soul.

Fire signs

People are spontaneous, impulsive and apply their energies to its fullest. Their life principle is evident as enthusiasm, spirit, active, inspired, faith, encouragement, self-expression, out-going, emotional and a lively imagination.

Earth Signs

These people acts slowly, quietly and calmly as the reaction. They are sensual, grounded, and emotion-full and tend to change slowly. They are likely towards the physical forms and are practical enough to improve the material world by utilizing it.

Air signs

They are intellectual, conceptual, and quick, animated and apply their energies in diverse ways. These are found with mind's sensation, perception, ideas and expression in the personal and social interaction.

Water Signs

These people have empathy, cooling and healing sensitivity with others. They are highly imaginative, nurturing, introverted and deeply emotional rooted in their lives.

Elements and Modalities

To understand the various patterns of forces is to evaluate them in terms of their modalities. Each of the four elements have three modes in three vibrational modalities—Cardinal, fixed and mutable. Cardinal denotes- Creative and active, Fixed symbolize- maintaining and preserving, Mutable connotes- adaptive. Assimilating and synthesizing.

Cardinal Signs

These people are self-starters and doers. They symbolize the direction of initiating movements of energy and get things progressively. However, people with few planets under this sign face trouble in the swift of things.

Fixed Signs

These people sustain and preserve life. They syndicate the concentration of energy accumulated inwards toward a center or radiating outwards from a center. They are at the center of things and resolutely refuse to go along with change. However, people with few planets under this sign are short of persevering and the ability to follow through.

Mutable signs

These people are correlated with flexibility and constant change. The people under these signs are adaptable, indecisive and transformative. They integrate, communicate and assist things to change. Also, they are deeply receptive and affected by the surroundings.

However, people with few planets may face problems being flexible or adaptive to changes.

Elements and Groups

Traditionally, elements are tell apart into two groups—Fire & air, and water & earth. Fire and air are well-thought-out active and self-expressive. Whereas, water and earth are measured passive, receptive and self-containing.

This differentiation proves beneficial as a whole to the birth charts so as to make a distinction about the individual's energies and method of self-expression instead of taking a broad view over the qualities of all the people indiscriminately in certain category.

Each sign of particular element allude to dissimilar expressions, elemental energy, and levels of development as well as the relationship of energy. The zodiac signs classified to each of these groups of elements have the fact that signs of the same element and element in the same group have a preference of being compatible to each other.

Astrology and Signs

What are zodiac signs?

The signs are the energy patterns that syndicate specific and detailed qualities of an individual. The zodiac is a circular belt of space in the heavens consisting of the manoeuver of orbits and planets including the luminaries-sun and moon. The zodiacal circle is divided into twelve parts and is termed as the signs of zodiac.

The different planets of unlike nature are continuously travelling through the zodiacal circle thereby exerting an influence on the nature of signs according their separate characteristics.

Fire signs- Aries, Leo, and Sagittarius

1. **Aries (March 21 to April 20)**

You are the first sign of Zodiac. You are a born leader and shine bright in a crowd people. You take initiatives fearlessly in everything and discover the unknown in life. You are lively, dynamic, active, courageous and fighter too.

You are impulsive, concentrated and spontaneous and often act first and think later about your actions & reactions. You are your own boss and control your destiny. You are adventurous and admire independence of expression. You hate laziness and accept all the challenges with passion. Your greatest strengths are confidence, self-assurance and target-oriented. However, sometimes these strengths make you self-centered.

Aries are attention-getting, aggressive and competitive. Aries have the urge to 'Be'. If you can learn to balance your patience and sensitivity with boldness and determination, you can transform your life magically and you will be much loved by your near & dear ones!

Symbol- The Ram, Ruling planet-Mars, House- 1, Number- 1, Gemstones- Diamond and opal

2. Leo (July 22 to August 23)

Sun, your ruling planet, is located at centre and so is you-golden globe! You are dynamic, energetic, and generous and want the best in life. You urge to 'express'. You are creative, expressive and have pride and ownership. You love to act, play, romance, children and sporting.

Leo is dignified, dramatic, flamboyant, radiant, loyal, joyous and playful. You are aggressive, confident and outgoing. You are good at expressing in theatres and arts. You have a big heart and love animals too.

Symbol- lion, ruling planet- sun, house- 5, Number- 5, gemstones- peridot, jade, sardonyx and diamond

3. Sagittarius (November 22 to December 21)

You search for truth, religion, philosophy, ideology and for the unknown things. You are bountifully enthusiastic, religious, generous, jovial and optimistic. You are profound, frank, expansive, aspiring, abstract, prosperous and humorous. You look for wisdom and are very direct & to the point. Sagittarians are good natured, tolerant and magnanimous. You are always welcomed in politics and communities because of your philosophical and far-reaching energies.

Symbol- archer, ruling planet- Jupiter, house-9, number-9, gemstone- lapis lazuli, turquoise and onyx.

Earth signs- Taurus, Virgo and Capricorn

4. Taurus (April 20 to May 21)

Taurus is about having, responding and valuing. Taurus is steady, deliberate, determined and response to life's new ideas and impulses. These are fixed, practical, solid, aesthetic, resourceful, methodical, sensual, dependable, retentive and private.

You look for pleasure, comfort and security. You love to create and nurture physical forms of beauty and bring forth growth and development. Taurus is gentle, loyal, steadfast, determined, accepting, mothering and provides a base to possess and acquire things.

Symbol- bull, ruling planet-venus, house-2, number-2, gemstones- emerald and sapphire

5. **Virgo (August 23 to September 23)**

These are concerned with conservation, salvage, harvesting, repair and maintenance. They are urged to serve and rules initiation and apprenticeship. Virgo is skilled and knows the use of craftsmanship, tools, analysis, organization and discrimination. These are busy, careful, systematic, concerned, discerning, self-sacrificing, worrying and practical.

They love to serve. Ordering and organizing are the prime focus of this sign. They are compassionate and responsive, martyr and often concentrate on others rather than themselves. They always want perfection.

Symbol-virgin, ruling planet-mercury, house-6, number-6, gemstones-sapphire, zircon and agate

6. Capricorn (December 21 to January 20)

Capricorns are concerned with achieving the long term goal or plan. They are clear-seeing, practical, ambitious, disciplined, reserved, cautious, skeptical, restrictive, sober, orderly, controlling, and manipulating. However, they are unemotional and un-tolerant. Capricorns are focused on their career and reputation. Capricorns believe in hard work and are logical.

They attain mastery and success and tend to become improved and more enjoyable with the passage of time and age.

Symbol-sea goat, ruling planet-Saturn, house-10, number-10, gemstone- garnet and emerald

Air signs- Gemini, Libra and Aquarius

7. Gemini

They have an endless search for experience, knowledge, limits and boundaries. They love to be in motion, communicating, inquiring, investigating and exploring. They are often nervous, versatile, inventive, curious, changeful, quick, reasoning. Gemini looks to learn and communicate.

They love to make connections through letters, telephones, speech, thoughts, writing and mental processes. Gemini is verbal, mental and restless, independent.

Symbol-twins, ruling planet-mercury, house-3, number-3, gemstones-alexandrite, agate and amethyst

8. Libra (September 23 to October 23)

It always surrounds marriage and partnership. It seeks balance and harmony. It focuses on the principle of unconditional acceptance or response. They are diplomatic, compassionate, attentive, appreciative, attractive, cooperative, considerate, compromising.

They need union, reconciliation and balance. It desires for love and beauty. They are god-gifted artists, mediators and facilitators, peace makers, intelligent and communicative. They do not like coarseness and social gracious. However, when faced any challenge proves 'iron fist in velvet glove'.

Symbol-scale, ruling planet-venus, house-7, number-7, gemstones- opal, sapphire and jasper

9. **Aquarius (January 20 to February 18)**

They carry the spiritual light of ideals into actuality. Aquarius is impersonal, willing to work with anyone holding same aspirations. They like team work. Aquarius is aspiring, revolutionary, individualistic, futuristic, eccentric, rebellious, humane and idealistic.

They seek to transcend, freedom and equality. They symbolize humanitarian goals, idealism and altruism. Aquarius is always non-partial and non-sectarian. They focus on such goals that are advantageous to many people. They value individualism, freedom and equality. Aquarius are innovative, intuitive, discoverer and unconventional and genius too!

Symbol-water bearer, ruling planet-Uranus, house-11, number-11, gemstone-amethyst and bloodstone

Water signs- cancer, Scorpio and Pisces
10. Cancer (June 21 to July 22)

Cancer is homesick people and loves to be t house or home. They are emotional, protective, domestic, sympathetic, responsive, dependent, caring, moody, supportive, and comfortable.

Cancer is the mother of zodiac protecting and providing for others. They are sensitive and emotionally bonded in relationships. They seek feelings, trust, security, comfort and nurturance.

Symbol-crab, ruling planet-moon, house-4, number-4, gemstones-ruby, pearl and moonstone

11. Scorpio (October 23 to November 22)

They seek transformation, adjustments in marriages or union, sharing of resources, emotions and intimacy and the changes made by those sharing. Scorpio needs elimination and purification by removing the excess. They are penetrating, purging, powerful, compulsive, intimate, ecstatic and cathartic.

They are motivated by power. Scorpio is passionate, intense, magnetic, charismatic and personal. However, they are found secretive about personal feelings. They are excessively possessive and jealous and face trouble in letting go. They need spiritual nature or socio-political power.

Symbol-scorpion or phoenix, ruling planet-Pluto, house-8, number-8, gemstone- topaz, pearl, citrine

12. Pisces (February 18 to march 21)

They seek to surrender. Pisces is compassionate, vulnerable and intuitive. They are a nature of trust, imaginative, receptive, mysterious, mystical, psychic, inspired, vague, elusive and knows sacrifice. They get the motivation from unity, inner truth, and values.

They are deeply rooted to spiritual and psychological. Pisces is very understanding, patient and long-suffering. They often misunderstood the things. They are kind hearted and forgive easily. They are easily moved by the feelings of surrounding people and are escapist!

Symbol-fishes, ruling planet- Neptune, house-12, number-12, gemstone-bloodstone and jade

Astrology and Planets

What are planets?

Planets are the heavenly bodies that control the flow of energy and represent the factors of experience. Moon, Mercury, Venus, Sun, Mars, Jupiter, Saturn, Uranus, Neptune and Pluto.

In astrology, these ten planets are considered according to their size, proximity and influence on earth and thereby, to the humans, animals and matter!   Each of the planets has its own specific personality, energy, functions and susceptibilities.

The planets are important to study for the creation of birth chart. The sun and moon (planets in astrology) are important heavenly bodies present in every chart. At new moon, it is said that we begin, build, develop and receive new things and energy.

Sun

The sun tells us the inner self and spirit of a person. It reveals to us the general vivacity and ability to assert oneself. Its urge is to 'BE'. It is a mentor or embodiment of authority to which everyone looks up and receives. The sun is an enlightenment and insight of our-selves as a sovereign person and the center and initiator of own reality. It needs to be renowned and to express themselves.

Moon

The moon is known as the mother of planets deeply rooted with emotions and desire to generate security in the world. It feels an urge to inner hold up, domestic and emotional protection. Moon needs emotional harmony and a sense of belongingness. It influences our mobility, flexibility and adaptableness to change.

Mercury

The mercury has conscious, rational and logical mind. They represent an urge to express the opinions and intellect through skill and speech. They symbolize communication and establishing connections and relationships with others. Mercury is the messenger of God and thus, truth. It needs to learn and express verbally the ideas and thoughts by being reasonable.

Venus

What are planets?
Planets are the heavenly bodies that control the flow of energy and represent the factors of experience.
Moon, Mercury, Venus, Sun, Mars, Jupiter, Saturn, Uranus, Neptune and Pluto   In astrology, these ten planets are considered according to their size, proximity and influence on earth and thereby, to the humans, animals and matter!   Each of the planets has its own specific personality, energy, functions and susceptibilities. The planets are important to study for the creation of birth chart. The sun and moon (planets in astrology) are important heavenly bodies present in every chart. At new moon, it is said that we begin, build, develop and receive new things and energy.
Sun
The sun tells us the inner self and spirit of a person. It reveals to us the general vivacity and ability to assert one-self. Its urge is to 'BE'. It is a mentor or embodiment of

authority to which everyone looks up and receives. The sun is an enlightenment and insight of our-selves as a sovereign person and the center and initiator of own reality. It needs to be renowned and to express themselves.

Moon

The moon is known as the mother of planets deeply rooted with emotions and desire to generate security in the world. It feels an urge to inner hold up, domestic and emotional protection. Moon needs emotional harmony and a sense of belongingness. It influences our mobility, flexibility and adaptableness to change.

Mercury

The mercury has conscious, rational and logical mind. They represent an urge to express the opinions and intellect through skill and speech. They symbolize communication and establishing connections and relationships with others. Mercury is the messenger of God and thus, truth. It needs to learn and express verbally the ideas and thoughts by being reasonable.

Venus

Venus symbolizes love, sharing, cherishing, sensuality, attraction, harmony, grace, beauty and compassion. Venus is responsible for seeking beauty in your life, sharing with friends and lovers, nourishing art, creative eloquence and music to your soul. It has an urge for being societal and love, fondness and happiness. It needs soothe and harmony and desire to be close to others.

Mars

Mars represents passion, energy, courage, determination, dedication, spontaneity and drive of a person to explore and adventure new experiences. Mars are impulsive to take actions and aggressions. They have an urge to act positively, self-confident, and aggressive. They want to accomplish their requirements and needs physical and sexual pleasure.

Jupiter

Jupiter represents the life path, the way through, continuity and succession. Jupiter symbolizes path finder, good fortune, success and luck. It illuminates and guides through wisdom when there is darkness in life due to Saturn. Jupiter always grows and seeks adventure. It searches for faith, trust and confidence in life.

Saturn

Saturn syndicates moral conviction and conscience. It symbolizes the powers of fortitude and the ability to concentrate and create structures that serve our highest prospective. It outlines maturity, discipline, good efforts and good use of resources. It has an urge toward safety and security through substantial achievement. It teaches responsibility, self-discipline and perseverance.

Uranus

It focuses on individualistic freedom and independence from self-ego and esteem. It has an urge towards delineation, creativity and reliance from tradition. It needs change, exhilaration and expression without self-control. It stands for intuition, inspiration and insights. It is a great awakener and inventor and seeks liberation.

Neptune

Neptune is the dissolver of restrictions. It is kindhearted, sensitive, holy and the guide and spiritual mother. It seeks for trust and faith and lay down arms to the universal anonymity of unity. It has an urge to break away from the boundaries of one's self and the material world. It symbolizes free-will and union.

Pluto

Pluto has an urge towards total renaissance and penetrates to the foundation of experience. It symbolizes self-refine and needs to let go of old plans. It searches for transformation, transmutation and elimination. Pluto shows how we compact with power, personal and non-personal anguishes. Pluto is the lord of underworld- death and rebirth.

Other Celestial Bodies
Besides these planets, astrologers pay attention to the several other heavenly bodies like asteroids- Chiron, Ceres, Pallas, Juno and Vesta that influence with a minor effect to the people. In Our solar system, planets revolve around sun in the same direction but some of the planets are seen moving backwards sometimes. This retrograde motion of planets is also studied by the Astrologers.

Mars

Mars represents passion, energy, courage, determination, dedication, spontaneity and drive of a person to explore and adventure new experiences. Mars are impulsive to take actions and aggressions. They have an urge to act positively, self-confident, and aggressive. They want to accomplish their requirements and needs physical and sexual pleasure.

Jupiter

Jupiter represents the life path, the way through, continuity and succession. Jupiter symbolizes path finder, good fortune, success and luck. It illuminates and guides through wisdom when there is darkness in life due to Saturn. Jupiter always grows and seeks adventure. It searches for faith, trust and confidence in life.

Saturn

Saturn syndicates moral conviction and conscience. It symbolizes the powers of fortitude and the ability to concentrate and create structures that serve our highest prospective. It outlines maturity, discipline, good efforts and good use of resources. It has an urge toward safety and security through substantial achievement. It teaches responsibility, self-discipline and perseverance.

Uranus

It focuses on individualistic freedom and independence from self-ego and esteem. It has an urge towards delineation, creativity and reliance from tradition. It needs change, exhilaration and expression without self-control. It stands for intuition, inspiration and insights. It is a great awakener and inventor and seeks liberation.

Neptune

Neptune is the dissolver of restrictions. It is kindhearted, sensitive, holy and the guide and spiritual mother. It seeks for trust and faith and lay down arms to the universal anonymity of unity. It has an urge to break away from the boundaries of one's self and the material world. It symbolizes free-will and union.

Pluto

Pluto has an urge towards total renaissance and penetrates to the foundation of experience. It symbolizes self-refine and needs to let go of old plans. It searches for transformation, transmutation and elimination. Pluto shows how we compact with power, personal and non-personal anguishes. Pluto is the lord of underworld- death and rebirth.

Other Celestial Bodies

Besides these planets, astrologers pay attention to the several other heavenly bodies like asteroids- Chiron, Ceres, Pallas, Juno and Vesta that influence with a minor effect to the people. In Our solar system, planets revolve around sun in the same direction but some of the planets are seen moving backwards sometimes. This retrograde motion of planets is also studied by the Astrologers.

Astrology and The House

What is house system?

The astrological house demonstrates us which spheres of life obtain more weight than others in a horoscope. Each astrological house stands for a specific phase. The house division of a horoscope contrasts from person to person as it is measured according to the time of birth and the geographic position of the place of birth.

The horizon- Ascendant and Descendant

This axis that divides the horoscope into an upper and a lower half symbolizes the horizon at the time of birth. The point at which the eastern horizon traverses the ecliptic is called the ascendant.

Planets found near the ascendant at the moment of birth are rising. It is the commencement or cusp of the first house. On the other hand, the descendant is found on the cusp of the seventh house. The planets close to the descendant are setting.

The Meridian- imum coeli and medium coeli

The other significant axis in house division is the meridian. This split the horoscope into an eastern and a western half. The highest point of juncture of this axis with the ecliptic is called the Medium Coeli or mid heaven. Planets near to the Medium coeli dwell in the highest possible place in the heavens at the time of birth.

The lower point under the horizon is called the Imum Coeli. The planets near the imum coeli dwell in the lower side of the earth.

1st House

The sign at the beginning of the first house notify us about someone's qualities, temper and foundation. It symbolizes our interpretations, immediate, inborn response and demonstrates how we represent ourselves to the world.

2nd House

The second house revolves around communication and its inhabitant enlightens us about the material circumstances, the greedy urge and how we pact with possessions and materialistic ways. This embraces the connection to our own body.

3rd House

The third house and the planets involved tell us of our siblings and the mode in which we communicate on an on a daily basis level and the relationships which decide our everyday life.

4th House

This house depicts our origins, the parental home and the state of affairs persuading childhood and youth. It describes how we communicate to family, our attitude towards father, heart and home.

5th House

Sexuality and eroticism are at fifth house, along with all types of creative appearance. This house also portrays how we relate to children, pleasure and fun in life.

6th House

The sixth house illustrates the situations neighboring us in our daily lives, including the work atmosphere and daily practice. This includes our deeds towards subordinate people. Physical hygiene and care also feel right here, as well as tendencies to certain obtained sickness.

7th House

The descendant sign and planets involving the seventh house tell us about how we select our soul-mates and explain the partnerships and relationships we look for.

8th House

The eighth house gives you an idea about how we narrate to communal goods and how we deal with material loss. Traditional astrology maintains that this house has an affinity to death and all things metaphysical. Death would then be the ultimate material loss and the study of metaphysics can be a very distinguish way of dealing with this loss.

9th House

The ninth house describes our spiritual leaning, life philosophy and our world outlook. These are often prejudiced by journeys to foreign countries. The attitudes cultured and formed in this house can greatly sway matters of the 10th house.

10th House

This house is of particular importance as it affects our choice of profession and our sense of calling. This continues all through our lives. According to custom, and experiences, this house expresses the relationship with mother.

11th House

The eleventh house describes how we relate to friends, supporters and mentors. This house shows how we speak about the society in which we survive.

12th House

This house represents those phases of life in which the individual no longer plays a part, where we step back for a better whole. Astrology sees hospitals, prisons and psychiatric institutions in this house. It is also associated with monasteries.

Astrology and Aspects

What are Aspects?

The vigorous connections between the various energies of life are represented on the individuals by the aspects in a natal or birth chart. These aspects are the angular distances between the planets in a horoscope, measured as angles within ecliptic circle.

These interactions influence the working of planets together. Aspects are the lines of force amid diverse energy centers, planets, in energy fields recorded by the chart. The aspects are calculated within the 360 degrees circle, revealing the energy fields in the birth chart. Aspect among planets creates either easiness and is considered as gifts or frictions which are put up in challenges to triumph over.

Aspects and Groups

Aspects are categorized in two groups.

Disharmonious or challenging aspects

As the name suggests, the disharmonious aspects creates bad effects and stress in life. It refers to the major aspects that are opposition (180 degrees), square (90 degrees), and minor aspects include grand cross, quincunx (150 degrees).

Harmonious Aspects

As the name suggests, the harmonious aspects are considered superior. It refers to the trine (120 degrees) and sextile (60 degrees) which are the major aspects. The minor aspects includes quintile (72), bi-quintile (144), semi-sextile (30 degrees).

Major Aspects

Opposition (180 degrees)

This major aspect is regarded as disharmonious or dynamic. It has a encouraging and revitalizing effect. The quality of the aspect depends on the planets caught up. As a whole, an opposition stuck between two planets creates tension among them with positive results.

Square (90 degrees)

The square is regarded as a disharmonious aspect as the planets implicated appear to be blocked. The tribulations that take place from the square keep on turning bad. The complexity lies in trying to bring together two forces that are trying to move in completely dissimilar directions. As a rule, this takes the form of desires and requires which are equally limited.

Trine (120 degrees)

The Trine is a harmonious aspect where the planets effort mutually in a gracious manner by enriching each other. Trine give you an idea about where your natural talents lie and it depends on you in what way you make use of your talents. The planets in Trine support each other. They allow you to accept others, yourself and the circumstances.

Sextile (60 degrees)

The Sextile have a harmonious effect that totally depends on the planets involved. Sextile also explores your talents and ease like the trines but, trines come very naturally to the individuals whereas sextile are very overt to the native. Sextile are outgoing and relationship-friendly aspects. They disclose the potential and capabilities for intelligent use of energies.

Conjunction (0 degrees)

The conjunction is a harmonious aspect and depends on the planets involved and how near the aspect is. Planets and points that outline a conjunction are energies that are unified. They are merged and proceed collectively. For example, if the distance between mercury and sun becomes less than a few degrees then mercury will burn! As a whole, conjunctions show an instantaneous relationship that works in one way or another.

Minor Aspects

Quintile (72 degrees)

The quintile tends to be a harmonious but minor aspect in which planets involved are at a distance of 72 degrees. The planetary energies connect you to your inner and outer self by using your inherited capacities and insights, termed as spiritual astrology.

Bi-Quintile (144 degrees)

A bi-quintile is a minor and harmonious aspect to mental place, where planets involved are at a distance of 144 degrees which is double the quintile aspect. This helps you to stride into master consciousness and acknowledge your latent potential for mastery.

Semi-sextile (30 degrees)

The semi-sextile is a harmonious minor aspect where planets involved are at a distance of 30 degrees and has a less impact than a sextile. The two planetary energies are associated but they influence each other obliquely. It can express a lack of ease and may manipulate the development of your welfare. **It has the capability to make you conscious of your innate personality.**

Grand Cross

The grand cross is a disharmonious aspect where planets are positioned at 90 degrees apart. It is the most entrenched and secure pattern, giving amazing sensual, practical, and psychic insight. The universe revolves around a stable structure. It can be a basis of power and firmness, but also may tend to be self-defeating due to the push for going in a number of directions at once, thereby going in no direction.

Quincunx (150 degrees)

The Quincunx is a disharmonious and minor aspect where involved planets are 150 degrees apart. This aspect implies a need for adjustment or a change of approach. The planets concerned share nothing in common, so it is a very hard aspect to integrate into our being. The only way of altering the disharmony of this aspect is to reliance one's inner voice so that one can go ahead into transformation and incorporation.

Astrology and Horoscopes

What is the difference between Astrology and Horoscope?

Horoscope is merely a blue-print of your actions, a birth chart or natal chart that contains interpreted things about your-self. On the other hand, Astrology is a 'science of stars' that evident itself through studying, analyzing, understanding and interpreting the horoscope.

What is Horoscope?

The word horoscope has emerged from Greek words 'Hora' and 'scopos' connoting 'time' 'observer'. The horoscope is an astrological chart or diagram that corresponds to the positions of the sun, moon, planets, astrological aspects and susceptible angles at the time of an occurrence like the birth of a human being. The other names of horoscope are- Natal chart, radix, sky-map, cosmogram and so on.

A horoscope is said to be an astrologer's interpretations based on the planets and sun signs. Although, there is no scientific proof of the accuracy of horoscopes and the techniques used in setting interpretations are well thought-out pseudo-scientific. To prepare a horoscope, three types of information are required- Date of Birth, time of birth and place of birth.

What horoscope enlightens you?

In our life, we learn a plethora of subjects on various topics- mathematics and science, literature and languages, geography and history, arts and many other subjects in schools and universities. However, we are not taught much about ourselves and each other which can lead to a contented and gratifying life ahead. To know ourselves we need to study horoscopes! It doesn't promise to forecast your future incidents but it reveals your personal traits that what kind of person you are.

A lot many people lives inside just one person. Sometimes you feel cheerful but sometimes you are sad and want to be left alone. Sometimes you are serious & thoughtful and sometimes you crave fun! These variegated sides of you are the signs of sun, Moon and planets at your birth to make you live to your best with these diverse visage.

The horoscope gives you an idea about the exceptional connection between the Sun, Moon and planets at the time and place of your birth. A horoscope channelizes you to find the right path of your life by showing the sights of your talents, conscious, feelings and the things that delight you.

Personalities via Planets

- The Sun depicts our desires for the deepest aspirations in life.
- The Moon tells us our emotional values and feelings.
- The Mercury reveals how we think and express ourselves.
- The Venus shows our relationships and communications with others.

- The Mars represents our capability to make use of our energy and talents in attaining our dreams.
- The Jupiter gives an idea of our enjoyment and understanding.
- The Saturn illuminates our self-discipline and strength of character we have in ourselves.
- The Uranus demonstrates our creativity, inventive, naturalist and originality.
- The Neptune explains our helping behavior to others that how we help each other.
- The Pluto makes us know the ways we can grow through intensifying our self-knowledge.

How Horoscopes Work?

The horoscopes serve as a map of heavens consisting of interpretations that are calculated to forecast the personalities of every individual. Horoscopes are designed and planned in accordance with some concepts – Native, celestial sphere, plane of the equator, plane of the ecliptic, plane of the horizon, angles, houses, zodiac signs, placement of planets, and aspects.

These components are already explained in the previous chapters in detail.

Health, Career, and Marriage Through Astrology

Health and Astrology

'A sound mind resides in a sound body'. Health is termed as perfect when every organ of the body as well as mind works powerfully without sickness and injury. For a nourishing and good health, the environment in which we live plays a vital role. According to Astrology, all the phases of life of a human being are controlled by the twelve houses, including health. Each of the twelve houses represents our body organs and the bad effect of malefic planets on these twelve houses creates health problems for that specific organ.

Houses and Diseases

- First house: Mind, face, head, appearance and complexion, total health, long life and skull.
- Second House: Right eye, throat, neck, teeth, mouth, gums, gullet and larynx.

- Third house: ears, arms, hands, shoulders, right ear and nerves.
- Fourth house: breasts, chest, lungs, stomach, elbow joint.
- Fifth house: belly, heart. Body strength, spine, liver, Spleen.
- Sixth house: digestive system, kidney, large intestine, colon, uterus and anus.
- Seventh house: glands, renal system, buttocks, adrenals and private parts.
- Eighth house: scortum, pelvis, seminal vesicles, sex organs, venereal diseases, ovaries, prostate gland.
- Ninth house: hips, thighs, knees, joints, bones, hairs and back.
- Tenth house: knees, joints and bones.
- Eleventh house: calves, left ear, left arm, circulation, legs, teeth, ankle.
- Twelfth house: left eye, lymphatic system, feet, teeth.

Depression and Stress

Today, stress and depression have become common problems in everyone's lives. It becomes a serious matter if depression strikes you frequently and holds you in its grip. According to Astrology, depression and stress is caused due to the malefic effects of planets on houses.

The first, ascendant, indicates brain and the way our brain thinks and react. The wrong placement of ascendant and the bad aspect of malefic planets create stress and state of depression in life.

The fourth house is for mental peace, happiness and comfort. If the fourth house is faulty, then it is void of power and creates a stressful and depressive life.

Also, moon necessitates our life with emotions. If moon is creating bad effects in the sixth, eighth and twelfth house, conjunction of moon with malefic planets, Saturn aspects moon, hemming of moon between two malefic planets, and moon posited with sun are the reasons for depression and stress.

Astrological remedies for health & depression disorders

Gemstones are represented as powerful weapons against the weak planets to benefit and improve health disorders in life. Each planet has a gem stone according to color that attracts the cosmic energy of that particular planet. In primordial period, gems were worn by kings in crowns with a faith of wealth, prosperity and protection from malefic planets.

Gems as well as the ashes of gems are used to treat various diseases. Gems are attractive, metaphysical, optical, healing and cosmic remedy to provide strength t the weak planets. But, remember, gems should be worn by consulting an experienced and knowledgeable astrologer.

- Blue Sapphire: Help in curing Bone and knee problems, rheumatism, paralysis, insanity, lack of energy.
- Red Coral: Help in curing acidity, indigestion, stomachs, fever, small pox, lack of energy, piles, boils, and measles.

- Ruby: Help in curing bones, blood pressure, heart problems, rheumatic pains, lack of confidence, unstable mind, and poor eyesight.

- Pearl: Help in curing improper sleep, depression, insanity, weak mind, indigestion, asthma, tuberculosis, heart problems, menstrual disorders and weak eyesight.

- Diamond: Helps in curing urinary problems, weak uterus, diabetes, weak reproductive organs, sexual relationships and urinary tract infection.

- Emerald: Helps in curing asthma, insanity, mental disorder, epilepsy, weak mind, stomach problems, gastritis, pancreatic problems and insomnia.

- Hessonite: Helps in curing asthma, insanity, mental disorder, obsessive disorders, epilepsy, weak mind, stomach problems, leprosy, insomnia and other diseases that are hard to diagnose.

- Cat's eye: Helps in avoiding mishaps, secret enemies and accidents. It cures obsessions, insanity, mental problems, urinary problems, paralyses and stomach problems.

- Yellow Sapphire: It helps in curing liver and kidney problems, gouts, jaundice, hernia, obesity, rheumatism and heart problems.

Career and Astrology

Today, a number of people are lagging behind in their bright future and career. In spite of possessing a good education, skills and qualification, most of the aspirants fail to get job. Astrology says that selection of accurate career is the foremost thing you should do. Astrology helps in finding the right choice of career for people so that they can acquire a perfect profession. The study of planets, Astrology helps in getting job as well as promotions in jobs for those who are already in job.

Houses and Career

Each House has its own importance in the career. The planet indicates the perfect profession for a bright career that should be considered by the person. You can read the zodiac signs (chapter 2) for knowing about your qualities, career and powers. The placement of strong planets in various houses represents the perfect career.

- First house: It indicates success in field of self-employment.
- Second house: It indicates career in banking, investments, finance, teaching, consultants, writing and publishing.
- Third house: It denotes communication, marketing, salesmanship, advertising, computer, web designing, travelling, writing and import-export.
- Fourth house: It represents land and vehicles, agriculture, building, sale and purchase of vehicles, mining.
- Fifth house: It explains marketing, brokers, finance, education.
- Sixth house: It syndicates loan, police, litigation, livelihood, court, loan-recovery, clinics.
- Seventh house: business and partnership, trading.
- Eight house: Insurance, research, astrology, magical powers.

- Ninth house: It represents luck and religion. Career includes law, priest, head of religious body, and travel to religious places.
- Tenth House: Career includes government jobs, politicians.
- Eleventh house: all planets here give good results. It represents income from various sources.
- Twelfth house: foreign countries, import & export, travel agency, hospitals, prisons.
-

Remedies to improve career

In astrology, Saturn necessitates significance in career and professional life. It gives troubles in life as well as in the career. If the Saturn is laced wrong in your chart, such problems will occur. But, don't be dishearten as Saturn causes only delay and hurdles, not denial. Saturn is a great mentor that makes you understand from the difficulties and failures. It is the Saturn which has the potential to give everything back in future.

The tenth lord plays an important role in making a perfect career. Tenth lord in Ascendant shows self employment, in second house it ensures career in teaching and banking sector. The tenth lord in third house syndicates communication, publishing and computer field. Its presence in 4th house represents real estate business, agriculture and mining. The tenth lord in fifth house indicates investment in stock market, legal advisors and military sector. Its plays a great role in the seventh house by showing success in partnership.

The tenth lord in eight house depicts research as career and ninth house as pilgrimage, tours, professors and lecturers in institutes. Its presence in the tenth house promises job in government officials and management fields. The tenth lord in eleventh house indicates profession related to finance or trade and twelfth house as medical and foreign profession.

Thus, the lord of tenth house should be made strong to obtain success in career and profession. For the achievement in employment as promotions, blessings of

Lord Saturn should be taken to gain victory. The people who seek profession in lawyer, politics and educational institute should make the Jupiter strong to achieve triumph.

On the other hand, keep scenery of mountains or hilly area on back side of seat in the offices. In respective of all the professions, your seat should never be under a beam. Never face directly towards wall while you are sitting in a chair. It emits positive energy and positive results on your career.

Marriage and Astrology

Marriage has always been a concern for all those who doesn't get a life partner or a suitable match. Ages passes and many of the people get deprived of the marriage and its happiness.

Today, marriage has become a difficult part for the eligible person and parents too due to the increasing education and expertise and expectations in life. The life is much complex and competitive that makes delay in marriages.

Moreover, the marriage charts do not match and due to the non-compatibility again, problems occur in fixing a marriage.

Love marriages

It is always preferred to consult an astrologer and to match the horoscope charts before fixing a marriage. Besides, in the present scenario, love marriages are getting recognition and acceptance worldwide.

Astrology says that love and romance is indicated when Venus is in union with the Ascendant and is laced with fifth, seventh or eleventh house. Astrologically, fifth house in horoscope indicates love and romance. Seventh house belongs to spouse and the relation between the seventh and fifth house results in love marriage.

In love marriages, exchange of lords and aspect of benefice Jupiter makes the love marriages stable. However, the lack of faith, divorce is the results of malefic

Rahu, Mars or Saturn bringing disharmony and breaking of relations.

Remedies for successful marriages

- An auspicious result will emerge if benefic planets are placed in seventh house. If malefic planets are placed in the seventh house then it will be an inauspicious situation for marriage and hence, delay in marriages will occur.
- Saturn plays a main role in delaying the marriage.
- Harmony and bliss will be seen if the lord of seventh house aspects its own house.
- If malefic planets are placed in the eight house of horoscope, longevity of spouse suffers and so match making should be carried out with caution.
- Jupiter gives bliss of marriage in particular houses in horoscope.
- Mars plays an important role in giving happiness and harmony in marriages. If Mars is placed in first, fourth, seventh, eighth or twelfth house of

horoscope, it is not an auspicious match and should be taken out carefully.

- The position of planets in tenth and third house represents good or bad relationship with the in-laws and brother-sister-in-laws.

- After consulting the astrologer, gems should be worn to make strong your weak planets related to seventh house so as to get success in marriage.

F.A.Q.

1) What can Astrology do for me?

Astrology is a guideline to help you throughout your life. The sun-sign and birth-chart does not define who you are but help in explaining and knowing the personality traits. From choosing a path of career to love, romance and marriage, astrology plays an important role in leading you to the accurate direction. The horoscope signs reveal a new way of thinking in you by making you understand about your inner-self in a more and better way.

2) Does my astrology chart reveal my "fate"? Do I have any choice about what happens to me?

Astrology explores your likelihoods, possible life-experiences which derive naturally from your personal astrological temperament. A good astrologer can also tell you when those experiences will occur and advise how to handle them gracefully. Remember- *'If you know what kind of creature you are, then you know how you should live'.*

3) **If Astrology is so great, then why some predictions go wrong?**

Astrology tells the behavior of human beings and their actions. The life of humans is very complex and so is to decipher the influence of planets and stars. Astrology gives a very accurate picture of human being's life if explored by a learned astrologer. If the predictions go wrong, then do not doubt astrology, but the astrologer.

4) **Can Astrology Predict Future?**

Your present actions are a reflection of your past deeds. The future depends on present actions and there lies a connection between past, present and future. An astrologer can understand the past, present and future of humans and can reveal your previous birth to you. And so, Future can be predicted through Astrology.

5) If I don't have the birth details, how can I know about my future?

To know about your future, birth time, birth lace and birth date are of relevant importance to know about your horoscope. But, if you lack these details, then it is better to know your traits and future through Palmistry which can make predictions from your palms.

6) If everything is destined by god, then how astrology help me?

By the help of Astrology you can change only a few things in your life that are allowed by God depending on your past deeds. Astrology explores those areas and gives guidance to take the necessary correct steps to hold maximum benefits. Various things cannot change as they are decided by God and no one can change them.

7) **My friend and I are the same Sun Sign, why are we so different?**

When creating a personalized chart, the position of the all the planets are studied in shaping the psychological composition of an individual, along with the Sun. The individual planets move at dissimilar speeds and will be at various parts of the zodiac as time moves on. So if two people are born on the same date with the Sun in the same position, the other planets won't be in the same

position. This is necessary as the manoeuver of these other planets will change the analysis of the birth chart as well as the personalized forecasts.

8) How can the planets cause things to happen here on Earth?

Few astrologers believe that the planets actually cause anything to happen here on Earth. "The idea that the cosmos is a unity and that all parts of it are interdependent was central to the alchemists of times past and is still central to the quantum physicists of today. Linked to the idea of unity and interdependence is the concept of macrocosm and microcosm". This means that all happenings by the universe are also reflected inside every individual. Science confirms that each human being actually contains all aspects of the world around them − including those of the plants, animals, minerals and celestial bodies.

9) **If my birth star is not compatible with that of my prospective partner and hence we should not marry?**

To decide whether two people marry or not is judged by an astrologer through the planetary compatibility of horoscopes of both girl and boy who want to marry. A single factor like 'star' and 'yoni' alone not decide for a suitable match. For a match, Ashta Kootas, eight factors- Varna, vashya, taara, yoni, graha, bhakoot, naadi all should be seen.

10)What about Twins? They are born on the same day, location and almost the same time?

Twins are born on the same day and time, their horoscopes would be the same and so the influence of planets and stars will be same on them.

However, the difference in the quantity will be seen in the twins

thereby the individual competence and ability to receive energies

varies from one person to another that totally depends on the actions

of previous birth and revelation to present social conditions.

Conclusion

It has been said that "What is the point in astrology if you cannot change your destiny? Well, it's true that you cannot change your destiny, but still it helps knowing about gravity". Astrology is the connection of us with the cosmic energies for our betterment.

Astrology does not articulate any judgment. Just like nature, it has no good or bad. It has no prejudice for any race, religion, sex, gender, traditions or nationality. It just divulges what was, what is, and what can be! To consult and study astrology is to know about your personal traits-what are your likes? What is your weakness? What is your strength? What troubles you? What is beneficial for your health? What path you should take? What kind of soul-mate will understand you? What profession will lead you to success?

There are numerous questions that prevail in everyone's mind. All the replies can be obtained by astrology. But it is important to look for a learned astrologer who can make accurate interpretations about you by reading your natal chart.

This book is a key to open the doors behind which you are barred! This book will help you generating an urge to seek astrology and investigate yourself. It will let you know the answers to the 'why' of everything within the territory of human survival.

Though astrology often encounters with scientists but it is termed as a pseudo-science. Astrology is about dwindling confusions in life and mounting clarity. It should be studied and explored with a view that it is more about understanding than belief; it is a knowledge system not a belief system.

According to Plato- 'A life unanalyzed is not worth living'. Astrology is an amazing means for self-introspection and self analysis.

Just start today to know yourself in a deep and better way!

88040268R00044

Made in the USA
Lexington, KY
05 May 2018